DON'T PLAY THE GAME

A Manifesto of Disengagement

Dr. Arnaud Prevot

Introduction

There is a predominant malaise that exists in our world. We have long ago given up religion as a people, and we have replaced it with all sorts of different activities, approaches, philosophies, and ideologies in order to search for something that gives us meaning. This malaise comes with an antidote. Society and those who help run it have given us a **series of stories** that, when used properly, will allow us to thrive and reduce this feeling of unease.

The stories that we have been given no longer work, and it can be said that they never really worked. There is no way to relieve ourselves of the unease that permeates every part of contemporary life, yet the **authors of the stories** continue to insist that the stories have merit.

This book is a call to a better future. It is not in the marketplace competing with other concepts or competing with other strategies. This book does not engage in the Marxist discussions of power, and it does not engage in the Capitalist discussions of value.

Progressives have lost. Revolution is not possible, at least not anymore. The entrenched moneyed interests are here to stay, and they have won. The tools of politics are ineffective because the power has corrupted those who were looking to change the world, in fact, people have no concrete idea as to what they want the world to look like.

Conservatives have lost. Far too many have given up on the idea of freedom, they no longer want it anymore. People have voluntarily given up religion, traditionalism, and *Traditional Values*. They live according to what makes them feel good (sensate), and will buy their way into whatever they want, feel like and desire.

What this manifesto is attempting to explain is that **active disengagement** from numerous facets of our contemporary society is all we have left. It is the only tool left to assert our sense of individualism and self, whatever the politics we hold. It is the last arrow in the quiver of self-determination, and it is the final ability for us to exert ourselves as human beings.

You've read the rules of the game, you understand that you *could* thrive in the game, but that most people lose. People have come before you and attempted to play it. We never hear about the game's many losers, we only hear about the small minority of winners. When society hands you the dice, hold them tightly in your hand and utter the words of Melville's Bartleby the Scrivener: *"I would prefer not to"*.

Don't play the game!

1. Towards the human as a product.

Our homes are crammed with things that we don't need. We overeat, we overwork, we overstress. This leads us to feel entitled to overplay. We watch too much television and spend hours on social media scrolling through the world's most mundane and digitally curated information. It's not politics or culture, but a slanted view trying to get you to vote, buy, consume, and think a certain way.

The political cycle is always on and the presidential campaign season lasts over two years. Every election is the "most important" and every candidate is "evil", "bringing us backwards" or "ushering in the change we need"...etc. We've seen it all before.

People are no more... we are "useful idiots" or "innocent victims". We are consumers and voters, polluters or racists. The person as an individual has no more merit, but is part of a block to be convinced, sold to, derided, marketed to, rejected or pandered to.

It's no wonder we no longer seek freedom... structural or systemic freedom. We have become hopelessly seduced and addicted to pigging out on convenience, luxury and consumption.

It wasn't always that way, the economy of attention may be the defining characteristic of late-stage capitalism, but we started nobly and with an economy that focused on filling our needs. In the 1940's, when the world converted a War economy into a production economy, when the soldiers and officers of the war came back and used the same processes to start mass-production... We were a needs-based economy. You only bought what you needed. Thrift and caution were still the norm, and this was buttressed by strong savings rates during the war years.

Then came the post-war boom of mass consumption and marketing. This led to another consumption dimension for the middle and lower classes... wants. The want-based dimension has only been for the upper-classes until then, but from the 50's onward, we saw most basic human needs met for an increasing number of people in the US. This led businesses to develop a new approach. Thanks to the marketing innovations from thinkers like Edward Bernays, Ivy Lee and Philip Kotler, we pushed past the idea of consuming as values based, but consuming as identity. This led to the needs-wants mix. But there was a story or narrative that we were told to follow... *satisfy needs first, and then maybe you could satisfy your wants... but don't forget to save money too.*

Slowly, there began to be a growing number of people who lived this story *in reverse*. They failed at meeting their needs and looked to satisfy their desires first. Many of their friends and family undoubtedly advised them to "take care of business" first, but to no avail. You may know people like that... with toys, tools and goods in their home, but not enough money to pay for their child's education or healthcare. This is usually accompanied by rationalisations in their lives... "I've got it under control" was the motto.

This was where companies needed to step in and stop their pervasive marketing approaches. It was obvious that some were more susceptible to the marketing campaign than others... too much so. But the companies did nothing, because there was too much money to be made. This is where they failed to pass business-ethics muster.

The 1980s and 90s saw an increasing wave of mass consumption and the creation of a new flagship for the economy. This was the rise of *Finance*. Goods and services people needed and wanted were no longer enough, people were to place themselves in large and leveraged debt for the chance of winning it big in the future, either with higher earnings from education (with student loans), scaling up businesses (with often times government-backed business loans) and with increased home prices (with mortgages). People made money from bets and numbers were often created out of thin air. This was partly due to the deregulation and the suspension of the gold-standard.

The early 2000s led to yet another economics paradigm, *the individual as product*. Technology companies began to offer numerous products for free to the entire world. Free email accounts, free word processing, free blogs, free spreadsheets, free communication programs, free video conferencing, free entertainment...etc. Few, if any, of the happy digital consumers asked how all of this was being paid for. Where was the product?

It's us.

Technological applications chop up our lives and sell our multi-dozen characteristics to the highest bidder so that we can be provided ads in return. We are the product and the companies are the "new consumers".

We pay with our attention.

We have 24 hours in the day, the longer we can interact with a tech-based brand or service, the more money the technology companies make, the more the beast grows.

In 1917, the top 5 biggest companies were characteristic of the needs-based economy:

1. US Steel (Shelter)
2. AT&T (Communication)
3. Standard Oil (Energy)

4. Bethlehem Steel (Shelter)
5. Armour and Co. (Meat, Food)

By 1967, the top 5 biggest companies were characteristic of the wants/needs based economy

1. General motors (Automobile)
2. Ford Motors (Automobile)
3. Exxon Mobil (Energy)
4. General Electric (Consumer Goods)
5. Chrysler (Automobile)

By 2017, the top 5 companies were indicative of the attention/ person-as-a-product economy

1. Apple (Computers/Software, Info. Services)
2. Google (Computers/Software, Info. Services)
3. Microsoft (Computers/Software, Info. Services)
4. Amazon (Goods Fulfillment)
5. Facebook (Info. Services)

What is the future going to bring? Perhaps a world where we own nothing and where we are fed, entertained, dressed, housed, educated and kept fit through a new all-encompassing system. We are seeing traces of this today.

We are told that we own a phone and we pay a monthly subscription to a phone plan. But we don't own it, it's built to only last 2 years and it will take that long to pay it off. It may be in our possession, but we cannot opt to not pay, since it is useless without a SIM card and access to a cell-network. We no longer own the media that we have "purchased", since we subscribe to a streaming service. We no longer own our higher education (Higher Education or otherwise), we "rent" it. The practical skills we need for employment are changing so much that we are required to engage in "official life-long continuing education" as part of our employment.

We do not own our homes, as we spend a lifetime paying off mortgages, only to be sold and exchanged for others when the time comes.

We do not own our identity, since we are threatened daily with sophisticated technological identity theft and attacks.

We no longer own our likeness, since we are at the mercy of a world of Deep-fakes and doctored images and media. Even when a video is real, people acting inappropriately can simply say… "It's a Deep Fake… it wasn't me".

These few examples (and there are many more) point to a large interconnected System which we will explore...

2. The Media-Business-Political-Educational System

The current world is led by a series of interdependent and interconnected feedback looks which has a flavor of *Corporatist Capitalism* at its center. This is to be distinguished with *Traditional Capitalism* by the fact that it specifically looks to benefit large corporations and their shareholders.

The system acts like a *human body* in the interdependency that it showcases, with **Business** at its heart as we will see after defining some terms.

a. Business - "The Heart"

This is loosely defined as the profit-making system dominated by a few large companies in each industry which looks to increase shareholder value and profit for itself. It is not a pure form of capitalism as it interacts directly with the Political system

b. Politics - "The Brain"

In this context, it is the three parts of the government which act to permit and/or regulate the Businesses. Some laws are even written by business and industry lobbyists themselves. Some large companies use regulation and their ability to digest it to discourage other companies from entering into the market and thereby keeping a larger share of the market in their industry. This has a consequence of failing to keep the large companies in check by having to respond to a newer, more crowded market. Politics also acts as the Executive Functioning apparatus, determining regulation and deregulation along with tension and loosening up. Politics is also promoted by both Business and the Media.

c.   The Media - "The Mouth"

This encompasses the print, radio, TV and Internet organizations that are often owned by the Business companies themselves. Their stated intent is to push authenticity and objectivity as a way to ascertain the "Truth" and "determine what is really going on". Also, they will say that, since Watergate, they see themselves as a tool to *"speak Truth to Power"* and to *"expose lies"*. The dependency that the Media has with Business (their owners) often makes this goal unrealizable. This is seen by the fact that they have lost trust with the American people. In 1972, Gallup found that 72% of the population trusted the media, and by 2016 that number had collapsed to 32% [1]. Also in 2016, only 16% of Republicans trusted the Media. This loss of trust is coupled with the fact that as of 2018, journalists were the third least trusted profession in the US [2]. In the UK, we find 27% trust journalists, something Ipsos defines as a "record high". Lastly, the Media places itself physically in State, Local and Federal government buildings and cultivates relationships with politicians, community leaders, Educational leaders and business owners ("Sources"). All of this adds credence that the Media works more as a mouthpiece than a traditional arbiter of Truth.

d. Education - "The Memory"

This is the network of public and private schools in the US, from day-cares to graduate schools. They look to "instruct" and pass on knowledge. Over the last 50 years, they have shifted away from "creating a learned citizenry" to "educating the whole child". They often depend on the government (Public) and private organizations (Grant-making organizations and Businesses).

When looking at the trust factor, we are seeing that in 1973, 58% of people saw public education as favorable and in 2021 the number was 32% [4]

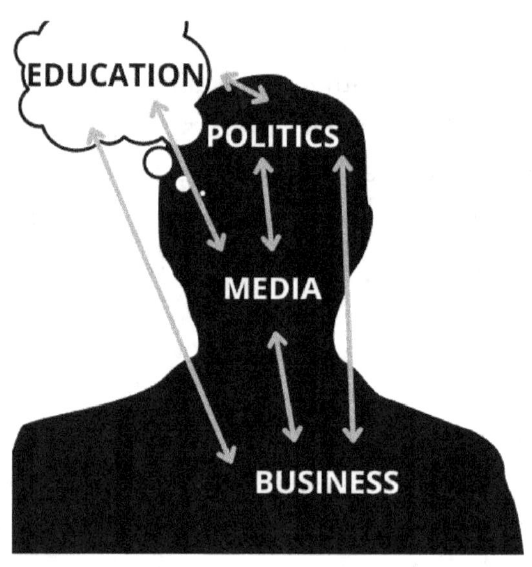

The System represented as a human body

This System is large and it is the stability of our time. In its mind, **nothing can be allowed to upset it or destabilize it**. It has stories that it repeats through Education and the Media as it looks to both *educate and "re-educate"* the members of the population. The predominant story is that this is in fact a benevolent system, since it was built as a response to the Soviet threat in the second half of the 20th Century, that it provides sustenance and meaning to the populace and that it "helps bring forth a well informed citizenry"

This System however, like all large scale overarching Systems looks to continue to grow, and recently, it is looking to morph. It is a shape-changing entity which can never fully be grasped, or comprehended. In order to continue to grow, it taps into the basest areas of the human spirit and psyche. One day it looks like our placenta source of nourishment and the other day it appears like a vicious cancer. In order to grow, it must control. In its mind, it's a benevolent form of control.

What is this System… early definitions included ideas like :"The Globalized-World", "The Post Cold-War-World Order", and the "Free World". While necessary to define the System, they are not sufficient since the System also encompases the real estate in our minds and consciousness.

Thomas Friedman, in his 1999 book The Lexus and The Olive Tree: Understanding Globalization, says of the all-encompassing Globalized world, we "can't see the world [and that we] can't see the interaction that are shaping the world, [so we] cannot strategize about the world". This is what the System counts on.

The System has one fear: not being able to grow or losing control. It has protected itself against this by tapping into a pattern in tribal humanity. **The system is encouraging our country's split in two.** Simply put, any opposition to the System is weaker if it is divided, and if the human libidinal forces are aimed at each other and not at it.

3. The Two Americas and the Origin of the Division

The System has taken advantage of very real human traits, such as tribalism, group think, cognitive biases and so on … **to split America in two**. It did not invent the idea of a split, but it pushes the division as a means of self-preservation.

This division has become so prevalent that it has metastasized into the economy. This split is very lucrative for many in the political and entertainment sectors. Let's dive deeper into the where the division began and where it is leading us to :

Ever since Aristotle declared that humans were "political animals", the idea of socio-political factions has existed. Mimicking our natural human and evolutionary sense of tribes/families, these political factions have revolved around numerous issues. Today, the struggle between the Right and the Left is central to almost every country in the West. The political conflict between the Right and the Left is central to today's modern Western Civilization with ideological roots going back thousands of years.

Such a division is present in the United States to such a degree that we are, for all intents and purposes, **two separate and collocated nations** with a large part of the nations having defined territories, cultures, histories, values, social systems, and politics.

Is this division of "the two US nations" anything more than the classic urban-rural or partisan divides? It is those two divides pushed to such an extreme that the idea of a single nation appears to have frayed.

So what are the characteristics of these two nations? SImply put they can indeed be classified as *Blue/Urban* and *Red/Rural* Americas.

Where does this split come from? It originates with the values split between the progressives and conservatives (and libertarians).

Social psychologist Jonathan Haidt performed scientific studies that found that there are six fundamental human values that we all share. However when looking at different political positions he found that conservatives, libertarians and progressives put extremely different emphases on these different values.[6][7]
A summary these values goes as follows:

(1)	**harm** : which says that hurting others is bad.
(2)	**fairness** : people should reap what they sow
(3)	**liberty** : the people shouldn't oppress their social inferiors and have the freedom to act as they please.
(4)	**loyalty** : having a sense of loyalty towards those in their group.

(5)   **respect for authority** : of various systems in society

(6)   **purity** : certain things are sacred and can't be violated

The results show that **progressives** are extremely high in the *value "harm"* (this is why left-wingers will say children are starving in Africa... *"how can we do nothing!"*). Afterwards progressives are interested in *value "liberty"* (caring about if people are oppressed by unfair hierarchies) which is a lot of where their emphasis on helping oppressed groups comes from. There is a little focus on "fairness", but almost no association with "loyalty", "respect for authority" or "purity". Progressives are more the far extension of the West's greater emphasis on harm reduction and liberty/libertinism that finds its roots all the way back in the Early Modern Era and the Industrial Revolution. It is during that time when a greater focus was focused on human institutions and a decline in the Church-focused groups and systems.

Conservatives, on the other hand, are pretty well balanced on all six values with high emphasis in all facets. It should be noted that conservatives are similar to the rest of the world, geographically and throughout history. In non-western societies for example, people are higher in authority, loyalty and purity than the coastal areas of the US.

Libertarians are interested primarily in liberty and fairness which is why libertarians want as little government as possible and are fine with prostitution, marijuana, and guns.

An interesting and fairly recent development is the social justice wing of the progressives has picked up a new attribute of extremely high purity in which saying the wrong words, or misappropriating is treated as an attack on the sanctity of their movement.

A **progressive** might think that a conservative's insistence upon national honor is inherently irrational. Consider the *Vietnam War*... For conservatives, the war made logical sense, as America could not be seen as not protecting its allies and letting Communism spread. However, for progressives, it was a war of colonial oppression in a useless country that American boys would die in. Similarly **conservatives** often view left-wing social spending on ideas like education and social programs as irrational given they have no direct economic output.

This example (as well as innumerable others) explains why when conservatives, progressives or libertarians argue with the other, their arguments often fall on deaf ears. A **progressive** might argue for gay rights since it's a representation of their harm and liberty functions, to help the oppressed. While religious. **Conservatives,** coming from a Christian background, would view it as an attack upon the Christianity that has held their civilization together for two thousand years... in other words as an assault on the purity function.

The modern left-right binary is a way of figuring out the *trajectory of Western Civilization in the post-Christian world.* For 2000 years morality and ethics were relatively easy, since one just referenced the Bible and tradition. The reason that the fight between the Right and the Left is so contentious is that , at heart, **it's become a religious war** and that both sides have what amounts to entire metaphysical views about how the world works, how history happened, and what the direction of Western Civilization **should be** going forward

The religious war example here is used to describe a comprehensive ideology that tells people how the world works, how they can be good people, and creates a community of social believers, provides ceremonies and passes on stories about their entire cosmology.

Religion doesn't have to be involved in the left-right dilemma. Consider Buddhism or Confucianism that are atheistic belief systems at their core or look at Communism, in which the certain dialectic of history acts exactly as a "god" would.

In the United States and in most of Europe, the dominant parties are both fundamentally **liberal** and their predominant presupposition is that **individual rights and the collective well-being is good and should be the dominant aim of society.**

Liberalism does have flaws however, since it doesn't deal with any of the other aims of religion: it doesn't tell you how to be a good person, build communities or deal with the heartbreak of death , the joys of childbirth and the like...

Liberalism was an extension of a pre-existing Christian civilization, whose foundations are dependent upon the idea that the **individual was the fundamental element of society**. That's a Christian concept, which presupposes the existence of a soul and that creates a value for human life. Also consider Catholicism and the Church, which broke up clans by banning cousin marriage thus making the West the most individualistic civilization in history. The decline in Christianity has also seen the decline in traditional liberalism wherever it's happened. Consider the rise of nanny states and decline in Free Market Capitalism coupled with the rise of leftist ideology after WWII. Or consider the rise of atheist ideologies like Nazism and Stalinism after WWI. Lastly this decline has also been seen in non-Christian nations like the general weakness of liberal regimes in places like Japan and India.

When it comes to faith and particularly Christianity, the **Left** takes the fundamental understanding of Christianity as Christ taught it that humans are *inherently good, but sinful* and that we just need to spread love and generosity in order to be in the Kingdom of Heaven.
This view was doubled down through the frame of Greek philosophy since the gospels were written in Greek which believes that humans

were largely inherently good and rational and the people were capable of *perfectibility* through rational thinking

The **Right** was part of the Augustinian worldview that came out of persian religions like Zoroastrianism and Manichaeism which held that the world was a battle between good and evil and that people had to fight against their own inherent evil and greed the structure of Christianity existed as a bulwark against people who were born in Original Sin this was a view that was propounded by Saint Augustine and became dominant across the medieval Catholic Church.

The **Right**'s view of a sinful and constrained humanity is generally that of medieval Christianity, while the **Left's** view of humanity being perfectable through logic and improvement is a view that came through the Renaissance and has grown larger across modern history.

The belief that humans are inherently self-interested allows **the conservatives** to deal with their ideological opponents more easily than the **Left**, which views their

opponents as inherently problematic at best and evil at worst. For **Leftists**, that believe that perfecting the human character is possible, being against their goals

means you're trying to hold back progress. This is historically why you've seen a greater degree of fanaticism on **the Left** or why **leftist** groups often succumb to radicalism or infighting. The belief in perfectibility is also why they often succumb to guilt since they judge themselves against abstract standards rather than real world examples.

American economist Thomas Sowell saw this split and described **the constrained and unconstrained visions of the world**. The *unconstrained vision* or that the **Left** holds is that people are inherently perfectable when naturally good and that *if there's a problem* in the world *it has to be someone's fault* given that human nature and the world is naturally good and fair, this is why when there's a disparity in something like *income range* between ethnic groups or between sexes and the like, **the Left** looks for an oppressive group like the patriarchy or racism, since in their worldview unfairness and inequality are *the exception not the norm.*

Progressive think that people are naturally good and perfectable and that the world is able to be improved (through conscious reforms that people who are cultivated, educated and sincere are capable of), making real progress in the world and improving the human race. For them, a *racist joke,* for example is slowing down the perfection of the human race, which will solve the rest of our problems and thus enhance and perfect humanity.

The Right believes that human nature is inherently self-interested, if not evil, and that society exists in order to keep back our inherent moral weakness. They don't believe human nature is perfectable and rather that *existence* is. It's a permanent battle against the forces of evil/chaos and that we need processes and organizations like Religion, property rights and capitalism *to hold back the demons* inside the human spirit. **Conservatives** believe that we're permanently on *the precipice of a dark age* and that we need to fight evil

The Left will view history as a *process of continual improvement.* For business interests, capitalism is a way of creating a fair system that operates independently of a powerful government and personal discretion for
the religious religion as a way of fighting the inherent sinfulness of the soul.

For **the Right,** the human race is incidental to the world and that factors like geography, pre-existing systems and the like are more important than human agency and human good will. Right-wingers don't trust experts and academics who they believe to be influenced by their own greedy self-interests but like people who have done well for themselves.

Even though it is sloppy, even though it leads to riots in the streets, looting, name-calling and division in our schools/families/lives, the **System has created this division by uprooting the notion of one America and by stoking pre-existing tribalism inherent to human nature**

To do this, it has used numerous tools. One such example is the siloing technological algorithms that are used in our main technology companies. Such algorithms look at what we like and feed much of the same back to us. Many have turned to Social Media to express their distrust, outrage, anger and disappointment with the System, but it has had no effect, in fact, it has only fed the technology companies and have made them stronger.

The reader may simply be asking: Can't I just vote the System away? Or at least limit its power by my choices in the business, political and intellectual marketplaces? Not exactly… Read on.

4. The Appropriation of Rebellion

Many readers may be thinking, why not choose the small business, rather than the large corporation? Why not vote for the lesser of two evils? Why not push for a more fair educational system and join groups that wish to push that idea? If this is what the reader wants, then so be it. But it would behoove anyone to understand that **this cannot and will not change the System**. Any thought of joining "grassroots" organizations looking to "change the System" or push for more "Systemic change" for whatever reason, is mistaken. The System is smarter than that. **It often has provided outlets of rebellion against itself**. It is so large that it has developed channels and mechanisms to avoid any change. **The System has appropriated its own opposition.**

This is all the more problematic since corporations are taking political, moral and social stances. This is angering and alienating more and more people who are looking to express their anger by purchasing alternative products from other companies. Most consumers are not aware that there are numerous companies that are owned by the same parent company. As an example [12],

a. Anheuser-Busch InBev owns 50% of the brewing industry. They are even acquiring small craft breweries. Opting for a Modelo instead of a Budweiser benefits the same company.
b. Luxottica owns 80% of the eyewear industry. Opting for Panama Jack instead of Ray Ban may seem like opting for a competitor until you realize that you are enriching Luxottica either way.
c. Intel owns 98% of the microprocessors setup in servers.
d. Pearsons owns 60% of standardized testing in North America.
e. Paypal owns 91% of the mobile payment industry. Opting for Venmo instead makes no difference since Paypal acquired Venmo in 2020.

The following are small examples of this appropriation:

a. When we can only vote for two real parties in an election. Pick one or the other, the System perpetuates.
b. When a single company owns the soda, and juice, and water options. You have choices, but you always enrich the same company.
c. When a ten multinational corporation own over 90% of the Global food supply chain, you have to buy into the System [7]
d. When the government designates "Free-Speech Zones" to channel protestors away from big events. They decide where you can have your Free Speech, supposedly guaranteed by the Constitution as a condition of being a citizen.
e. Companies encourage you to vent your political anger on Social Media

platforms. The more you engage with it, the wealthier the companies get.

When the tools of rebellion are made by the Business entities, "regulated" and permitted by the Political structure, integrated in our lives by the Media and Education... etc...

Rebellion is baked into the System, and "rebelling", protesting, writing petitions...etc only feeds it and makes it stronger.

The feeding cycle is always the same.

a. Something is started at any level of the System (Business, Educational, Political or Media) which upsets.
b. This leads to collective action through Social Media, letters written to the Media and to the Government.
c. This allows grand-standing and virtue signaling as Business, Educational, Media and Political leaders are seen as "embracing the Revolt" or rejecting it.

d. The Politicians get more visibility and more brand awareness; the Media gets more eyeballs on the screen or clicks on the computer; and the Business sector reaps the financial reward of the anger.

Next, consider the work "The New Spirit of Capitalism" by French sociologists Boltanski and Chiapello. THey tackle the question of rebellion against the System by asking why anti-capitalist critiques seem so impotent in the face of new forms of market-oriented business practice.

They suggest that we should be addressing the **crisis of critique** by examining the assumptions on which it is based. Via an unprecedented analysis of management texts that influenced the thinking of employers and contributed to the reorganization of companies over the last decades, the authors trace the contours of a new spirit of capitalism. From the middle of the 1970s onwards, capitalism abandoned the hierarchical Fordist work structure and developed a new network-based form of organization that was founded on employee initiative and relative work autonomy, but at the cost of material and psychological security.

They call the initial rebellion against the System : *The Artistic Critique.* This initial critique focused on the loss of autonomy, creativity and individuality. Management theorists and practitioners saw that this disconnect was causing economic issues so they shifted their approach and developed (what Boltanski and Chiapello called) the *New Spirit of Capitalism.* This new system provided more autonomy, individuality and creativity as a means to let employees express themselves more. Consider the following examples:

1) You are still working 12 hour shifts at Subway, but you are considered a "Sandwich Artist". You are an "associate" and not simply an "employee"

2) You are given a $4000 bonus for staying at a job that drains you to the core, because it would cost the company $5000 to find and onboard another employee.

3) Walmart gives you free, unlimited donuts while depriving you of quality health care.

This is the seeds of the System appropriating the rage and anger against it. Like the character of Diana Christiensen (Faye Dunaway) says in the 1976 movie Network says *"the American people want somebody to articulate their rage for them."* The System is both the cause of the rage **and** the somebody doing the "articulation".

For Boltanski and Chiapello, rebellion of all sorts is now what helps the System's bottom line. They conclude that we can't escape the System, some resistance comes from the System itself and other rebellions are ineffective or simply not worth one's time.

Lastly, in the 1982 French graphic novel series called *Le Transperceneige (The Snowpiercer)*, where the survivors of a post-apocalyptic climate event all live on a long train going constantly travelling around the world. They are organized along class lines with the wealthy living in opulence at the front and the poor scratching out an existence in the back. The poor stage a rebellion and reach the front, only to discover that the revolt was orchestrated by the train's leader to thin the train's population and keep it sustainable. The System had appropriated its own rebellion.

While all of this seems bleak, is there some chance that the world can be improved within the democratic process? Read on...

5. You Can't Change the World by Voting

Engaging in the democratic voting process is seen as a given. Ever since the Cold War, the United States stood for freedom, capitalism, liberty, and democracy. The bedrock of any democratic process is that any legal person gets one vote. This occurs in direct democracies, representative democracies, or any other forms that have existed throughout history. Individuals will exercise their right even if the democracy is not a direct one, like with the use of the United States electoral college.

This system of democratic voting can only work if there are democratic options presented to the voting electorate. In other words, while it may be true that individuals can vote, *who* is chosen from a whole different process. Throughout the democratic world, large political parties present their candidates in oftentimes undemocratic means, and the presence of money to influence the brand of these parties and their candidates begins to warp the minds of the potential electorate by design. In other words, enough money and a criminal can be turned into a saint. With enough big party will, partisanship in the minds of citizens can be stoked to the highest, and potentially dangerous levels.

This entire party-election system is funded with large corporate monies and continues to maintain the status quo held all the while giving the illusion of a possibility for change. By voting, you often go for **the lesser of two evils**, and help the system maintain the smokescreen of legitimacy. If with great fanfare you are presented with a choice of pizza, hamburgers or fried chicken and told that it is your civic duty to choose between one of them, don't be surprised if you continue *to get ever fatter.*

Voting, unless it provides some level of *entertainment, distraction or pleasure,* must then be seen therefore as the act of what the Soviet Union called *useful idiots.* A pantomime way to *feel* engaged.

We should also remember that only half of the voting age population ever make it to the polls or send in their mail-in ballots. It is even fewer for young people, the disabled and non-whites. The solution for most individuals and organisations have been short on results at best and at worse continue to perpetuate the sclerotic and necrotic System. On the political **Right,** individuals who do not share the moral, America-centred, pro-business approach should be **discouraged from voting;** On the political **Left,** services and favour should be granted to those who do not already yet vote so that they can **increase the chance that the new voters will vote for them.** Each side is looking to disenfranchise the other side. Thus is the rational conclusion to a two-party zero-sum game. This is why no person can even expect political change through the democratic process.

But perhaps grassroots organizations that are looking to enfranchise more voters and stop gerrymandering of districts can help? Organizations like the *Brennan Center for Justice*

and REPRESENT.US are looking to bring conservatives and progressives together to uphold democratic values and limit actions like district gerrymandering. The latter's stated goals are to *"pass powerful state and local laws that fix our broken elections and stop political bribery. Our strategy is central to dismantling the root causes of inequities in our democracy, and ending political corruption, extremism and gridlock."* First, it should be noted that these organizations have **the right idea in theory** and that attempts to help the issue of gerrymandering, for example, have been tried before… such as having politically independent committees that redraw district lines. However, there are a number of reasons why this is unfeasible and unreliable, and why it will not change the underlying problem in the political side of the System:

1. Gerrymandering is an old concept, having started in 18th century England. When the colonists founded the US, gerrymandering started "almost immediately" according to Dr. Thomas Hunter, a political science professor at the University of West Georgia. In 1812, there was a backlash from the Federalists against gerrymandering, but when they won, they redrew the district lines themselves. It was then used by the Democratic party as a way to limit the power of the Black vote. The 1960s "Redistricting Revolution" decision by the US Supreme Court had Warren Burger's majority opinion state that all districts should be "roughly the same population". This decision coupled with the Voting Rights Act of 1965 seemed to strike a blow to the concept of gerrymandering. However, within a couple of decades, computer

technology made it easier for political operatives to strategically map districts to benefit their party under these new rules. Today, Hunter states that "in some ways **it's politicians picking their voters** as opposed to voters picking their politicians." This quick history shows us that all attempts to limit gerrymandering have failed because **it can't be fixed.** No one is above their own desires to see a party helped or inhibited when they are the ones drawing the district lines. Gerrymandering is baked into the American political system, it is older than the US and good-hearted men and women who look to eliminate it, realize its allure after they themselves get into power. In order to reform (or better yet, destroy it), one would have to reform human nature itself... the desire to see our own side win, the desire to give our side an advantage and the will of people to make such changes happen. Gerrymandering itself shows us that we are in a voting system that is deeply flawed and cannot give us the objectivity that it promises.[10]

2. The political System is only as good as the means to communicate it. Subjects need to be able to see their sovereign, without that, the latter loses mystique, it loses power. In the same way, politicians need to be seen and heard directly. **People will choose** which politics or which politicians they choose to listen to. What people read, listen to and watch becomes their political reality. This fact, coupled with the social media algorithms which only give people what they want, **makes two separate realities**, leads to an incapacity to reach any critical mass of people to affect political change whether done with the previously stated grassroots organizations or through the political process itself.

Lastly, the extreme political divisions are not conducive to compromise . The work of Kalmoe and Mason (2022) shows that 60-70% of partisans believe that members of the other party are "a serious threat to the United States and its people"; 40% say that members of the other party are "downright evil"; 15-20% say that the US would be better off is large groups of the other party "just died"; and 13-18% see violence as a justified action , if the other party won. [15]

"If voting made any difference, they wouldn't let us do it"
-Mark Twain

Perhaps the Media can speak "Truth to Power"?

6. In Media, "All news is Fake News"

What is the *Truth*? Truth is the complete, real, actual reporting of what really went/goes on in accordance with fact or reality. The one seeing the Truth needs to eventually disappear as their perception of the Truth is filtered by their uneven, biased and tainted mind. At best, the individual will be able to see a less-than-complete Truth. Therefore, the perceiver needs to do all they can to set aside comparisons, personal experience, narratives of their own mind and just *"be with the Truth"* in front of them. It will not be perfect, as it may begin to vere towards fakeness or partial truth. With the latter, a decision which needs to be made: *"What truth will we choose to leave in and what will we discard?"*. In academic study, the rigorous application of the scientific method allows for a deliberate rigid filter through which information can be fed and on the other side comes fact. Any limit or poor application of this method can lead to a low-quality process and outcome.

How is the News produced? There are too many events occurring to afford to send reporters on the scene, so first events are chosen, then reported on. It is usually fact-checked, edited and put to paper or on-air. In each of these steps we see a further and further distancing from the Truth.

Which event should we report on? The Editor-in-Chief or supervisor will make the call on this one. It usually has to be worth the time and investment of the news organization. The boss will take into account their own perceptions of what is important, filtered through their natural biases and experience. It can be assumed that a great deal of professionalism will be applied, and that others will be consulted (who all have their own biases and filters) and that the greatest good-will effort will be made. But everyone has a boss, and the supervisor will need to mind the mission of the news-organization and the explicit/implicit desires of the owners/readers/viewers.

The news gets reported. The reporter sent out will have their style, brand, tone and appearance. They will gather information and leave out some. They will choose what is important and what to discard. They will present their best good-faith effort, and will write to the best of their ability. It is their own filters and biases which will be actively at work without them knowing it.

Facts will be checked. Then comes the fact-checkers who will call up individuals in questions to verify the facts. More choices, more decisions, more information going through filters that will naturally leave things out and connect dots.

On the air or on paper. Then the information is distributed. The appearance of the news broadcaster, their tone of voice, the pronunciation of the names and words, their demeanour, the chosen order of the news stories ... all will influence how people will absorb the news and the underlying Truth behind it. It could be written for a newspaper, with word choices (like "controversial" or "mainstream"), writing style, writing tone all influencing the perception of the Truth behind the event. That Truth (at this point) has been filtered, cut, reworked, squeezed into multiple narratives (that of the Editor, news organization, advertisers). There will have been many decisions made. Remember that the word decision comes from the latin "scisere" meaning to "cut". Some things will be included, other things cut out.

It should be noted that editors, gatekeepers and human content filters see themselves as stalwarts soldiers against Fake News itself. "Without us fakeness will spread rampantly through the internet and people will not be able to know what is real or not" they will say. To a certain degree they are correct… However, who is going to protect us from them and their human failures? Everyone thinks that they hold a neutral perspective, but neutrality is not possible.

Returning to the definition that Truth is: *the complete, real, actual reporting of what really went/goes on in accordance with fact or reality;* then it can be concluded that, in spite of all of our efforts,: *"All News is Fake News".*

Is there anything we can do?

Many in the world of NGOs and similar organizations believe that educating the population is key to helping them determine what is real and what is fake news. It should be noted that they are often underfunded or part of the media system itself. Consider the podcast *On The Media* (onthemedia.org) and *Media Matters* (mediamatters.org). Both claim to be non-profit organizations focusing on media topics and the like, and they will clearly say that they have won *"numerous awards"* for *"independent journalism"* and *"media criticism"* but they are owned by Media parent companies or other entities located well within The System itself. *On The Media* is owned by WNYC New York Public Radio and Media Matters was founded by progressive activist David Brock as a specific counterweight to its conservative equivalent Media Research Center. The reader may ask why this is an issue. *Simply put, once cannot educate the issues with the media process and selection away.* While interacting with both the *Media Research Center* and *Media Matters* sounds like a balanced approach, most will not do it. This is because cognitive dissonance hurts [8][9], and people are naturally inclined to avoid that pain. This is also because most people have already curated (alone or with the help of a selection algorithm, like the ones found in Social Media) their media diet. Lastly, it's because the issues outlined in this chapter are still present, as long as the media process remains the same.

On The Media released its *"Breaking News Consumer's Handbook"* online, looking to help people navigate the media and become a better digital citizen. They obtained this list by talking with journalists from a variety of sources. It outlined numerous points to consider including:

1. IN THE IMMEDIATE AFTERMATH, NEWS OUTLETS WILL GET IT WRONG.

2. DON'T TRUST ANONYMOUS SOURCES.

3. DON'T TRUST STORIES THAT CITE ANOTHER NEWS OUTLET AS THE SOURCE OF THE INFORMATION.

4. BIG NEWS BRINGS OUT THE FAKERS. AND PHOTOSHOPPERS.

There are many issues here, starting with the fact that in an industry with such low trust, they are warning consumers to trust the media even less ("Wrong", "Don't Trust", "Fakers", "Hoaxers"). Secondly, they are essentially giving homework to individuals as they are looking for a way to conveniently consume their news. This leads most people to simply not bother with this type of debunking. Lastly, once these "media criticism" or "debunking" websites get established, they become the Media , at least in the minds of consumers and begin to suffer from the same collapsing trust mentioned above.

Media as a mouthpiece

In 1947, Robert Leigh edited a report called *A Free and Responsible Press* for *The Commission on Freedom of the Press [13]*. In it he expressed the following:

"The modern press itself is a new phenomenon. Its typical unit is the great agency of mass

communication. Those agencies facilitate thought and discussion. They can stifle it. They can advance the progress of civilization or they can thwart it. They can debase and vulgarize mankind. They can endanger the peace of the world . . . They can play up or down the news and its significance, foster and feed emotions, create complacent fictions and blind spots, misuse the great words, and uphold empty slogans."

This sentiment, coupled with Andrey Miroshnichenko's 2013 work called *Human as Media: The Emancipation of Authorship* where he said:

"Despite all the differences in social order between Russia and the US, the biggest American and Russian media are almost identical in their inclinations. They want to limit the distribution of important information. The Americans, for financial reasons, the Russians, for political (but also, in some ways, financial) reasons.

It turns out that the value of media is not determined by information, but by its absence among the audience. The media proclaim themselves a supplier, but it really serves as a valve, which opens for money or when given permission by the authorities...
The mass media's basic function is to eliminate diversity of opinion"

Both of the quotes illustrate the power of Media and its role. The latter is not an investigative arm looking to *"speak Truth to power"*, nor tell us what is going on in the world; it functions as a mouthpiece of the monied or political System and exemplifies what the term *propaganda* par excellence.

Is there any hope in our day-to-day lives? Any ability to push beyond the System and stand in Truth and reality? Read on...

8. Who are the Disengaged?

After the explanation above, it's important to clarify what the disengaged man or woman is not. The disengaged person is not a slacker or a hobo, they are not an anarchist or simply defined as "apolitical" although they hold certain aspects of each of these. He will find himself detached from most political questions, preferring to spend his time far more looking at concepts within his family, and his inner circle. It's not that he is selfish, but he is understanding that he has control over his own sphere, and nothing else. Contrast that with the engaged man who will who will relish reading and engaging in politics which fit his previously established beliefs and who will be "aghast", "bemused" and often angry at "the other side"

The disengaged woman will return to the market and focus on the immediate needs that she and her family have. She will be looking for quality over quantity, and will prefer to save a lot of money to buy one enduring product, one that may be passed on from generation to generation. That is the ideal. The disengaged woman will also focus on the events going on in her community and in her city rather than looking at national and international events. Her engaged counterpart will prefer quick, cheap and affordable products and attach to them a level of artificial value far above its objective status.

The disengaged woman will prefer to read primary sources rather than interpretation. If she does turn on the television, it will be for a very short amount of time to hear about an event, learning what happened, when it happened, and who made it happen. She will not look at "why" it happened. Knowing that as soon as one enters the "why?", one arrives in the realm of interpretation, and this is where a lot of the issues begin with the media. The exception to this comes from her own interpretation of the events. In contrast, the engaged woman will be seeking out "many opinions and interpretations" on the news to "help her put things into context"; she will gravitate more towards the interpretations with which she feels most comfortable. Selective secondary and "Critical" sources will allow her to avoid any cognitive dissonance in her intellectual approaches.

The disengaged man will reject broad identities and narratives, focusing on being a husband, father, believer, and nothing else. He knows that identities have often opened human beings to manipulation and unsubstantiated criticism. And he sees this as a tool of manipulation, and a tool of control. The disengaged woman will have a preference for the small, preferring to get to know the producers of the services and the products that she decides to purchase. Buying from pre-established relations allows for an increase in the quality that she seeks. Their engaged counterparts will establish their "selves" through their identities, and can often be found appealing to identity saying ... *"Well, as a ____________, I feel that...etc"*

The disengaged family have a preference towards homeschooling their children, not necessarily out of ideology, but out of accomplishing what they understand is their primary goal, passing on their own values to their children. If this cannot be achieved, a preference will be given to private education, as long as it provides active participation for the parents, oftentimes allowing them to teach a class. Contrast this with the engaged family who will hold that "a public education is key to a solid and engaged citizenry", and it should be supported.

The disengaged woman will have a unique relationship with her work, valuing flexibility and autonomy over status and money. The disengaged family knows that they will need to interact with the system on a regular basis, but they will never do so at the expense of their autonomy, integrity, and oversight. Interaction with the system should be a win-win situation. It should benefit the family as much as it benefits the System. If that balance doesn't work, the disengaged family will rightfully back away. The quest for disengagement is not a political statement. It is not a statement at all. It is a statement of human autonomy and an assertion of individual and familial rights.

As stated above, the disengaged individual is not a hobo or a slacker, but they do take certain characteristics of these to archetypes.

Much like the disengaged, hobos were seen as actively willing to work. They were not part of the communities in which they arrived, yet they were very polite, clean, helpful, and hard-working. Also, the 1990s understanding of slackers comes from the 1990 movie *Slackers* from director Richard Linklater. He said in a 1995 interview called "*Withdrawing in Disgust Is Not the Same as Apathy*" that simply defining slackers as lazy, simply *"hangin' out"* and doing nothing is a cheap definition. In it, he states that he "think[s] the cheapest definition [of a slacker] would be someone who's just lazy, hangin' out, doing nothing. [He]'d like to change that to somebody who's *not doing what's expected of them. Somebody who's trying to live an interesting life, doing what they want to do, and if that takes time to find, so be it.*"

The disengaged family will be seen as rejecting internationalism and globalism as a value system, all the while understanding why someone around the world would prefer their own culture to anyone else's. They will also reject any form of patriotism and nationalism as approaches that the System uses to push unnecessary engagement.

The disengaged family holds strong philosophical sympathies with Stoicism, Distributism, The Bruderhof, Minimalism, Cultural Libertarianism, Benedict Option and the Homestead movement; they will look towards Moral Natural Law to guide their beliefs and actions and many will be practicing believers in a traditional religion. They will differ from any political associations like Libertarianism in that they will not think that such an association will give them freedom, all the while being dependent on the System. They will instead take from the System what they need to survive and live and give no credence to any other part of it.

When it comes to history, the disengaged are suspicious of political labels assigned by modern historians and journalists to historical figures. They understand that *"last century's heroes are today's villains."* They will ask probing questions and understand the nuance of history rather than settle for someone's (even an expert's) opinion. Lastly, they are very hard workers who often prefer to work in small community institutions, small businesses or even work for themselves.

9. Engagement ruins your health and your relationships

Many who are reading this may ask themselves what issues come from media, educational or political engagement. They may feel like it is beneficial for them and that they can be part of a community or "society". After all, isn't our country founded on the participation of an active and well-informed citizenry?

The issue is one of a chasm between the theory and the practice. A University of Nebraska researcher named Kevin Smith performed a study of Americans' stressors and found that 40% say that politics is causing them anxiety, fatigue, loss of sleep and have cuased them to fracture their relationships. Smith also adds that 5% say than engaging in politics have left them suicidal. The study was conducted in two parts, once before the 2020 election and one after. The results were identical, showing that a change of presidents had no effect [16], even though Smith previously had thought that the issues came from Trump being in office [18] . These data were similar to another study Smith conducted in 2017 [17]. When looking at who was most negatively affected, it showed that they were "younger, lean Democrat, show more interest in politics, and actively engage more in political causes." [16]

Media engagement can also be detrimental to one's health. German author Rolf Dobelli, who wrote the book *The Art of Thinking Clearly: Better Thinking, Better Decisions*, elaborates in a Guardian article [19]. He starts off by explaining how we are keenly aware of the dangers of the overabundance of food, and that today, "we are beginning to recognise how toxic news can be." Dobelli continues by explaining how the news misleads us and warps our sense of risk. "News leads us to walk around with the completely wrong risk map in our heads," he says. Dobelli continues by illuminating how the news is irrelevant, asking us "out of the approximately 10,000 news stories you have read in the last 12 months, name one that – because you consumed it – allowed you to make a better decision about a serious matter affecting your life, your career or your business". The news is also mentally and cognitively toxic, as the constant stress of new and exciting stories triggers a flood of glucocorticoid or cortisol. Such an excess leads to digestion issues, nervousness, tunnel-vision, fear, aggression and suseptibility to infections. The news also feeds into our consistent confirmation bias.

"What the human being is best at doing is interpreting all new information so that their prior conclusions remain intact."
-Warren Buffett

Dobelli finishes by reminding us that the news wastes time and makes us passive, with story after story about overwhelming stories that we can do nothing about. This may lead us to develop a sarcastic and fatalistic worldview.

Engagement is not merely something done out of interest, but it can have a direct negative effect on one's well being.

7. The Last True Revolt; A Call to Disengage

To everyone reading these words, know that if the System works for you, if you feel fulfilled and enriched by it, *by all means enjoy it.* But to those who feel called to push beyond the System, beyond the control and to assert yourselves through your choices, let's consider the story of Herman Mellville's *Bartleby the Scrivener.*

This 1853 short story follows a Wall Street law clerk who is hired. After an initial phase of work, he suddenly refuses to do any work or perform any task asked of him by his boss, the lawyer… He simply answers *"I would prefer not to"*. Bartleby works alongside two other scriveners who are bewildered by the fact that he is present, but does not work. Eventually Bartleby finds himself on the steps of his former employer's building, laying down. He refuses all help and eventually dies in prison as a vagrant.

This may not seem like an optimistic view of a path forward, but let's consider a few points

1. Bartleby expressed his detachment by saying *"I would prefer not to"*. He doesn't say "No". He is suggesting another path where he maintains agency, and he is polite about it… *"I would prefer…"*. He respects

the lawyer, but asserts himself. There is no animosity in his words.

2. Bartleby chooses his path and flexes his *free will*, even if it contributes to his demise. The final words of Mellville's short story "*Ah, Bartleby! Ah, Humanity!*" express the absurdity of his death, but also his humanity. His humanity at having exercised his *Free Will* in the face of a disinterested and tit-for-tat world.

3. Bartleby was present in the world, he did not fight it. His body was present, but his mind was elsewhere. One can assume that he was thinking of a better place, or better things, of a better world.

Like Bartleby, remember that we are in this world, not of this world.

We simply need to stop paying attention, and most political turmoil, issues, and moral indignities will cease.

This is much easier said than done, as we have oftentimes wrapped up our identities with political, commercial or educational affiliations.

It is time that we radically disengage from politics at the top and refocus our eyes towards politics of the individual and family. Let's invert the pyramid of attention and rediscover our family politics.

It is time to radically disengage from Education and to learn not from illusion, not wishful thinking or interpretation, but from Truth and fact.

Let's rediscover the wisdom of the Scientific Method, as applied in the everyday and see it as the gift that it is.

It is time to radically disengage from and focus on the small, getting to know the producers of our goods and services directly.

Our interactions with them will allow for a greater sense of community and respect in our purchases will lead to better products being produced and lasting a lot longer than the mass-produced goods we have today.

It is time to disengage from the Media (Social and otherwise) on a regular basis so as to better integrate ourselves with our human natures and human relationships.

The primary and most important news comes from our family, and our social network is already established in our homes and communities.

Disengage with the System!

Remember that the poor passengers on the train in *Le Transperceneige (Snowpiercer)* preferred to blow up their train rather than continue to live in the only System they knew.

Know that you will be finding a form of freedom, some things that others will not know. But then a decision needs to be made, what is one to do with this *Freedom*?

This freedom can only be used to do what you should be doing. If one falls back into the realm of psychological and societal junk food, then exercising this disengagement will have been for nothing. Identify what you should do, from a moral, religious, societal, and economic point of view. You have been given the ball, now run with it.

"It is not the man who has too little, but the man who craves more, that is poor." - Seneca

With this detachment, and a strong desire to fill the void with moral and ethical actions, you will be able to identify nuance a lot better.

Without the yoke of the System, you will be able to empathize, attract, and get close to anybody. You will be able to sit down with an ideological opposite and hear what he or she has to say. You can identify common points of values with them and see them for the people they are.

Let the rational scientific approach be your guide. Let your love of a higher power move your soul.

Disengagement will bring people together, and paradoxically will leave them to engage in what really matters.

"The simple step of a courageous individual is not to take part in the lie."
- Aleksandr Solzhenitsyn

"You can resolve to live your life with integrity. Let your credo be this: Let the lie come into the world, let it even triumph. But not through me."
- Aleksandr Solzhenitsyn

As Solzhenitsyn says in these quotes, we can understand that societal lies will occur and

spread through our world, but we can take a
simple action: not take part in it.

Will this mean that we will lose out on
opportunities? The answer is unequivocal: *yes*,
but these were never opportunities that were
beneficial for us if they were anchored in
deceit and illusion.

Why eat the poisoned apple when we could
grow our own apple orchard?

Don't engage with the System to change your
life. Look to an authority higher than the
System, higher than yourself, higher than the
world !
Always remember to disengage with a
passion!

There are 2.25 billion families in the world
Start 2.25 billion revolutions!

"The right to vote has no impact. You can change the future of a nation more by how you raise one child."
- GK Chesterton

"It is no bad thing to celebrate a simple life"
-JRR Tolkien

"Weak people take revenge. Strong people forgive. Intelligent people ignore."
- Albert Einstein

"To live a good life: We have the potential for it. If we can learn to be indifferent to what makes no difference"
-Marcus Aurelius

"A man is rich in proportion to the number of things which he can afford to let alone."
-Henry David Thoreau, Walden

Be Rational, Be Responsible.
You don't know the power that you actually have...

Don't play the game!

References

[1] Gallup, I., 2021. *Americans' Trust in Mass Media Sinks to New Low.* [online] Gallup.com. Available at: <https://news.gallup.com/poll/195542/americans-trust-mass-media-sinks-new-low.aspx> [Accessed 28 November 2021].

[2] Statista Infographics. 2021. *Infographic: America's Most And Least Trusted Professions.* [online] Available at: <https://www.statista.com/chart/12420/americas-most-and-least-trusted-professions/> [Accessed 28 November 2021].

[3]

2021. [online] Available at: <https://www.ipsos.com/ipsos-mori/en-uk/politicians-remain-least-trusted-profession-britain> [Accessed 28 November 2021].

[4]
Gallup, I., 2021. *Education.* [online] Gallup.com. Available at: <https://news.gallup.com/poll/1612/education.aspx> [Accessed 28 November 2021].

[5] Nytimes.com. 2021. *Opinion | The Moral Chasm That Has Opened Up Between Left and Right Is Widening.* [online] Available at: <https://www.nytimes.com/2021/10/27/opinion/left-ri ght-moral-chasm.html> [Accessed 28 November 2021].

[6]
Nytimes.com. 2021. *Why Won't They Listen? (Published 2012).* [online] Available at: <https://www.nytimes.com/2012/03/25/books/review/ the-righteous-mind-by-jonathan-haidt.html> [Accessed 28 November 2021].

[7]
Business Insider. 2021. *These 10 companies control everything you buy.* [online] Available at: <https://www.businessinsider.com/10-companies-co ntrol-the-food-industry-2016-9#:~:text=These%20co mpanies%20%E2%80%94%20Nestl%C3%A9%2C %20PepsiCo%2C,dollars%20in%20revenue%20eve ry%20year.> [Accessed 28 November 2021].

[8]
Cleverism. 2021. *Understanding Cognitive Dissonance (and Why it Occurs in Most People).* [online] Available at: <https://www.cleverism.com/understanding-cognitive -dissonance-and-why-it-occurs-in-most-people/> [Accessed 28 November 2021].

[9]
Psycom.net - Mental Health Treatment Resource Since 1996. 2021. *Cognitive Dissonance: What It Is & Why It Matters.* [online] Available at: <https://www.psycom.net/cognitive-dissonance> [Accessed 28 November 2021].

[10] HISTORY. 2021. *How Gerrymandering Began in the US.* [online] Available at: <https://www.history.com/news/gerrymandering-origi ns-voting> [Accessed 28 November 2021].

[11] Petrek, Melissa; Hines, Alan (1993). "Withdrawing in Disgust Is Not the Same as Apathy: Cutting Some Slack with Richard Linklater". *Mondo 2000.* p. 81.

[12] Watchdog, W., Career, M. and Costa, C., 2021. *10 Companies You Didn't Know Had Near-Monopolies - Wall St. Watchdog.* [online] Wall St. Watchdog. Available at: <https://www.wallstwatchdog.com/money-career/10- companies-you-didnt-know-had-near-monopolies/> [Accessed 28 November 2021].

[13]
University of Chicago Press. 2021. *A Free and Responsible Press*. [online] Available at: <https://press.uchicago.edu/ucp/books/book/chicago/F/bo27983144.html> [Accessed 28 November 2021].

[14]
Jps.library.utoronto.ca. 2021. [online] Available at: <https://jps.library.utoronto.ca/index.php/nexj/article/download/35089/26867/87918> [Accessed 28 November 2021].

[15] *Radical American partisanship*. Nathan P. Kalmoe. (2021, August 12). Retrieved January 16, 2022, from https://nathankalmoe.com/radical-american-partisanship/

[16] Smith, K. B. (n.d.). *Politics is making us sick: The negative impact of political engagement on public health during the Trump administration*. PLOS ONE. Retrieved January 16, 2022, from https://journals.plos.org/plosone/article?id=10.1371%2Fjournal.pone.0262022

[17] *Stressed out: Americans making themselves sick over politics*. Nebraska Today | University of Nebraska–Lincoln. (n.d.). Retrieved January 16, 2022, from https://news.unl.edu/newsrooms/today/article/stress

ed-out-americans-making-themselves-sick-over-polit
ics/

[18] Anderer, J (2019, September 26). *A nation divided: U.S. politics taking physical, emotional toll on Americans*. Study Finds. Retrieved January 16, 2022, from https://www.studyfinds.org/a-nation-divided-u-s-politi cs-taking-physical-emotional-toll-on-americans/

[19] Guardian News and Media. (2013, April 12). *News is bad for you – and giving up reading it will make you happier*. The Guardian. Retrieved January 16, 2022, from https://www.theguardian.com/media/2013/apr/12/ne ws-is-bad-rolf-dobelli

www.ingramcontent.com/pod-product-compliance
Lightning Source LLC
Chambersburg PA
CBHW050048260726
48658CB00005B/1840